SCOOBY-DOO!

A SCIENCE OF MAGNETISM MYSTERY

by Megan Cooley Peterson
illustrated by Christian Cornia

THE MAGNETIC MONSTER

CAPSTONE PRESS
a capstone imprint

Scooby-Doo and the gang were at a concert by their favorite band, The Sound Magnets.

"Shaggy, what are you and Scooby doing?" Daphne asked. "Why aren't you dancing?"

"We're, like, using these magnets to try to find loose change," Shaggy answered.

"Roose range," agreed Scooby.

"We'll use our newfound moolah to buy some snacks," said Shaggy. "Good tunes really make us hungry."

"Of course they do," muttered Velma.

"But I think this magnet is broken," Shaggy said. "It won't pick up any coins."

"The magnet isn't broken," Fred said. "Magnets attract certain kinds of metal, like iron and steel. But they don't attract other metals, like copper and aluminum."

"What does copper have to do with finding coins?" Shaggy asked.

"Pennies have copper in them," explained Daphne. "In fact, most U.S. coins today are made from non-magnetic metals."

Shaggy scratched his head. "So, like, why does a magnet attract iron but not copper?"

"First you must understand how magnetism works," Velma said. "Magnetism is an invisible force, just like gravity. It can move a piece of iron without touching it. Magnetism starts inside atoms."

"What do a bunch of guys named Adam have to do with magnetism?" Shaggy wondered.

"**A-T-O-M**, not A-D-A-M," Velma said. "Everything in the universe is made of atoms, or groups of atoms called molecules."

"Tiny charged spinning particles called electrons orbit around an atom's nucleus," Daphne explained. "The motion of charged particles makes magnetic fields. Electrons in atoms have tiny magnetic fields."

"In most materials, like copper, the magnetic fields cancel each other out," Velma said. "This means there is no magnetic force."

"But in iron, the magnetic fields don't completely cancel each other out," Fred said. "Iron's atoms, therefore, are magnetized. In fact, many magnets are made of iron."

"Riron!" shouted Scooby.

"Yes, Scooby—iron," Daphne said.

"Like, I think he means that we're in the magnetic field of that creepy iron creature!" Shaggy cried.

FACT FILE

The ancient Greeks found rocks that could attract iron. The rocks were called lodestones. In ancient China, lodestones were used to guide ships.

Shaggy covered his ears. "The band sounds, like, a little out of tune!"

"A little?" asked Velma. "All the speakers are going haywire!"

"That creature is destroying everything on stage," Fred said.

"Look! It's getting away!" Daphne shouted.

"Come on, gang," said Fred. "Let's follow that mutant hunk of metal!"

"Here we go again," Shaggy moaned.

"Like, it's gone!" Shaggy exclaimed. "That's one fast metal monster. Can you find a scent trail, Scoob?"

"Ro rent," said Scooby, shaking his head.

"I'd say we've got another mystery on our hands," Fred said.

"You can say that again," Daphne agreed.

"I'd say we've got another mystery—"

Velma cleared her throat. "No time for jokes, Fred. Let's go question the band."

"I hope this investigation doesn't take too long," moaned Shaggy. "My coupon for free French fries expires at midnight."

Daphne knocked on the door. "No one's answering," she said.

"Maybe they went home," Shaggy said. "I say we do the same."

Suddenly the door creaked open.

"**Zoinks!** It's the heavy metal maniac!" cried Shaggy.

"Like, whew," said Shaggy. "We totally thought you were that metal monster."

"I'm Felix Fox, lead singer of The Sound Magnets. I was just trying on a costume for our next show."

Fred stuck out his hand and introduced the gang. "My friends and I like solving mysteries," he said.

"We can help figure out who, or what, destroyed your speakers and ruined your concert," added Daphne.

"That would be great," Felix said. "Please, come inside."

"This isn't our first run-in with that creature," Felix explained.

"Rit's r-rot?" asked Scooby-Doo.

Felix shook his head. "A few weeks ago, I received a text message. The message said the band had been cursed."

"Yeah," agreed the band's drummer. "And now that metal monster keeps showing up and sabotaging our shows."

"It must be hard to play drums with such heavy sticks," observed Shaggy.

"Those aren't my regular sticks," the drummer said. "My mom gave me iron drumsticks for my birthday. But one was stolen a few weeks ago."

"Let's go check out the stage and look for clues," Velma said.

"The speakers went haywire when that creature took the stage," Velma said.

"Why would that be?" Shaggy asked.

"Magnets!" exclaimed Fred. "Speakers use magnets to make sound."

"Fred's right," Velma agreed. "There are magnets inside every speaker. As electricity passes into the speaker, the magnets vibrate."

"The vibrating magnets move a cone made of paper or plastic," Daphne explained. "The cone sends out sound waves."

"I'm guessing the iron creature somehow used strong magnets to destroy the speakers," Velma added.

"Come on, gang," said Fred. "Let's see
what else we can find."

"What'd you find, Scoob?" Shaggy asked. "A snack?"

Daphne knelt next to Scooby. "It looks like pencil shavings. How strange."

"Our first clue!" Fred said.

"Watch out, Scoob!" Shaggy said, dropping his magnet.

"Look at that," Fred observed. "The shavings moved around the magnet."

"They're definitely not pencil shavings," Velma said. "If I had to guess, I'd say they're iron shavings."

"Those iron shavings must really like that magnet," Shaggy said.

"You're right," Daphne said. "Magnets have magnetic fields. A magnetic field is the area where there is a magnetic force."

"A magnet's two ends are called the north and south pole. The magnetic field flows from the north pole to the south pole," Fred said.

"And a magnet's magnetic force is strongest near its poles," added Velma.

strongest magnetic force

"Look, Scoob! Our magnets don't like each other!" Shaggy said.

"That's because a magnet's like poles repel each other," Velma explained. "But opposite poles attract."

"Just like me and hotdogs!" Shaggy exclaimed. "So does that have anything to do with those magnetic fields?"

"Exactly!" said Velma. "Remember that the magnetic field flows from north to south. When you place two like poles together, the magnetic fields repel each other."

"But when you place opposite poles together, they attract," Fred added. "That's because their magnetic fields flow in the same direction."

flow of magnetic field

S   N

FACT FILE

If you cut a bar magnet in half, the new pieces will have two poles—a north and a south. Each new piece that's cut in half will also have two poles.

"Any piece of iron can be made into a magnet," Daphne said. She rubbed Scooby's bar magnet along the iron drumstick.

"Ragic!" Scooby exclaimed.

"Actually, it's all because of domains," Velma said. "Inside each magnet are millions of micromagnets called domains. A magnet's domains are lined up."

"The domains in a regular piece of iron aren't lined up yet," said Fred. "Rubbing a magnet across the iron causes its domains to line up. The iron then becomes a magnet."

"We seem to be a magnet for that monster," Shaggy whimpered.

"We've got company!" Shaggy shouted. "And it doesn't look very happy!"

"Rot rappy," repeated Scooby, shaking his head.

"Look out below!" Velma cried. "The floor is falling!"

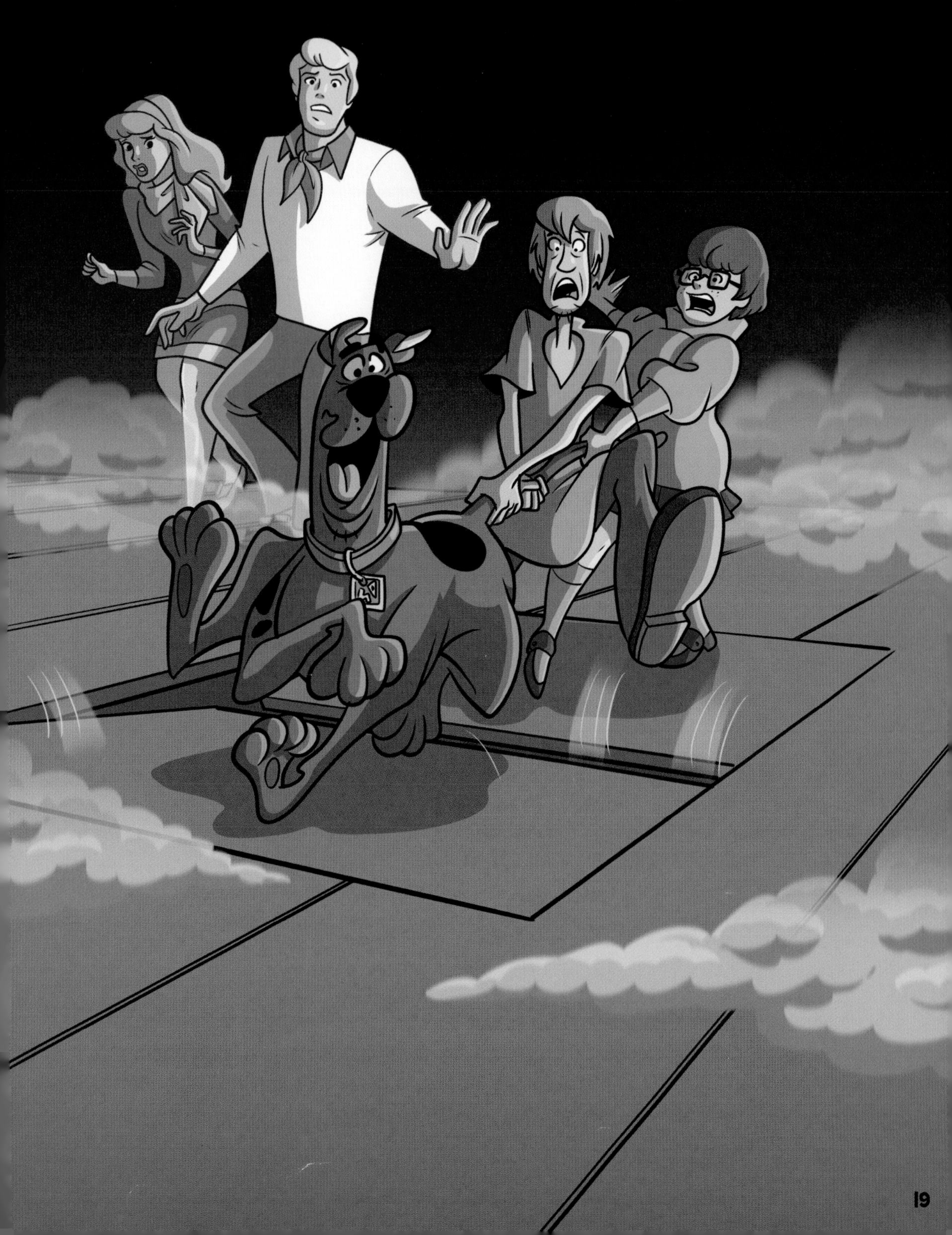

"Like, where are we?" Shaggy asked.

"We're in a some sort of tunnel below the concert hall," Velma said.

"What'd you find, Scoob?" asked Shaggy.

"Rore ravings," said Scooby.

Velma picked up some shavings. "Scooby's right. It's more iron shavings. Things are starting to make sense."

"Not to me!" Shaggy said.

"The creature has been using these old tunnels to appear and disappear," Velma said.

"I'd like to disappear out of this creepy tunnel," muttered Shaggy.

"Re roo!" agreed Scooby.

"Oh, great!" cried Shaggy. "How do we know which way to go? We'll never get out of here!"

"Actually, we will," Velma said, "thanks to my compass. I never leave home without it."

Shaggy looked at the compass. "How is knowing what time it is going to help us?"

"A compass doesn't tell time," Velma explained. "It uses magnets to tell which way you're going."

"Is the magnet like a map?" Shaggy joked.

"In a way, a compass is a map of Earth," Velma said. "Earth is like a giant magnet. The north pole of the compass magnet points to Earth's North Pole."

"Can your compass point me to the Burger Barn so I can use my French fry coupon?" Shaggy asked.

"Our work's not done, Shaggy. The front of the concert hall is north," Velma said. "That way!"

FACT FILE

Earth's magnetic south pole is near its geographical North Pole. That's why a compass' north pole points that direction. Opposite poles attract.

"Boy, are we glad to see you," Shaggy said to Fred and Daphne. "Next time, let's stick together like magnets."

"We found more iron shavings in a secret underground tunnel," Velma explained.

"And we found a trail of iron shavings leading to a junkyard," Daphne added.

"I've got an idea, gang," Fred said. "We can use a magnet to catch that magnetic monster."

"Where can we find a magnet big enough?" Velma asked.

"Follow me," Fred said. "We're going to the junkyard."

"I'll call Felix and have the band meet us there," Daphne said.

"I hope the Burger Barn is on the way," groaned Shaggy.

"We'll use this huge electromagnet to catch the creature," Fred said.

"Like, what's an electromagnet?" Shaggy asked.

"An electromagnet combines magnetism and electricity," Velma explained. "Without electricity, electromagnets lose their magnetism."

"Velma's right," said Daphne. "Electricity flowing through a wire creates a magnetic field. When you coil that wire around iron, the magnetic field becomes much stronger."

"Strong enough to lift the metal monster?" Shaggy asked.

"Turn on the power and we'll find out!" Fred shouted.

FACT FILE

In 1820 Danish scientist Hans Ørsted found that a current passing through a wire created a magnetic field. He had discovered the first electromagnet.

"**Jinkies!**" cried Velma. "Our monster magnet worked!"

"A little too well," said Shaggy. **"It's getting Scooby-Doo!"**

"Now it's time to see who this creature really is," Fred said, removing the monster's mask.

"Kirk? Is that you?" Felix asked.

"Do you know him?" Daphne asked.

"A few months ago he tried out to be the band's new drummer," Felix said. "But he needed more practice."

"Is this true?" Velma asked.

Kirk nodded. "If I couldn't be in the band, I decided there would be no band. So I used powerful magnets and water to short circuit their equipment."

And you stole the iron drumstick," added Daphne.

"Yes," said Kirk. "And I would've gotten away with it if it weren't for you meddling kids!"

"Well, gang, looks like we've solved another mystery," said Fred.

"Let's swing back by the Burger Barn on our way home," Shaggy suggested. "Burgers and fries go together like opposite poles of a magnet."

"Scooby Dooby Doo!" Scooby cheered.

THE END

GLOSSARY

atom (AT-uhm)—the smallest particle of an element

domain (doh-MAYN)—a group of magnetic atoms

electromagnet (e-lek-troh-MAG-nit)—a temporary magnet created when an electric current flows through a conductor

electron (e-LEK-tron)—a tiny particle in an atom that travels around the nucleus

force (FORS)—any action that changes the movement of an object

gravity (GRAV-uh-tee)—a force that pulls objects together; gravity pulls objects down toward the center of Earth

magnetic (mag-NET-ik)—having the attractive properties of a magnet

magnetic field (mag-NET-ik FEELD)—the area around a magnet that has the power to attract magnetic metals

molecule (MOL-uh-kyool)—the atoms making up the smallest unit of a substance; H_2O is a molecule of water

nucleus (NOO-klee-uhss)—the center of an atom; a nucleus is made up of neutrons and protons

pole (POHL)—one of the two ends of a magnet; a pole can also be the top or bottom part of a planet

repel (ri-PEL)—to push apart; like poles of magnets repel each other

SCIENCE AND ENGINEERING PRACTICES

1. Asking questions (for science) and defining problems (for engineering)

2. Developing and using models

3. Planning and carrying out investigations

4. Analyzing and interpreting data

5. Using mathematics and computational thinking

6. Constructing explanations (for science) and designing solutions (for engineering)

7. Engaging in argument from evidence

8. Obtaining, evaluating, and communicating information

READ MORE

Petersen, Kristen. *Understanding Forces of Nature: Gravity, Electricity, and Magnetism.* Mastering Physics. New York: Cavendish Square Publishing, 2015.

Thomas, Isabel. *Experiments with Magnets.* Read and Experiment. Chicago: Heinemann Raintree, 2016.

Winterberg, Jenna. *Electromagnetism.* Huntington Beach, Calif.: Teacher Created Materials, 2015.

INTERNET SITES

FactHound offers a safe, fun way to find Internet sites related to this book. All of the sites on FactHound have been researched by our staff.

Here's all you do:

Visit *www.facthound.com*

Type in this code: 9781515736998

 **Super-cool stuff!** Check out projects, games and lots more at **www.capstonekids.com**

INDEX

Thanks to our adviser for his expertise, research, and advice:
Paul Ohmann, PhD, Associate Professor of Physics
University of St. Thomas, St. Paul, Minnesota

Published in 2017 by Capstone Press, A Capstone Imprint
1710 Roe Crest Drive, North Mankato, Minnesota 56003
www.mycapstone.com

Library of Congress Cataloging-in-Publication Data
is available on the Library of Congress website.
ISBN: 978-1-5157-3699-8 (hardcover)
978-1-5157-3703-2 (paperback)
978-1-5157-3715-5 (eBook PDF)
Summary: A heavy metal monster at a heavy metal rock concert? Scooby-Doo
and the gang find themselves drawn to a magnetic mystery in which a creepy iron
creature is destroying everything in sight. Join their scientific investigation of the
magnetizing monster and help repel its powers!

Editorial Credits
Editor: Kristen Mohn
Designer: Ashlee Suker
Creative Director: Nathan Gassman
Production Specialist: Laura Manthe

The illustrations in this book were created digitally.

Printed and bound in the USA.
010051S17

OTHER TITLES IN THIS SET: